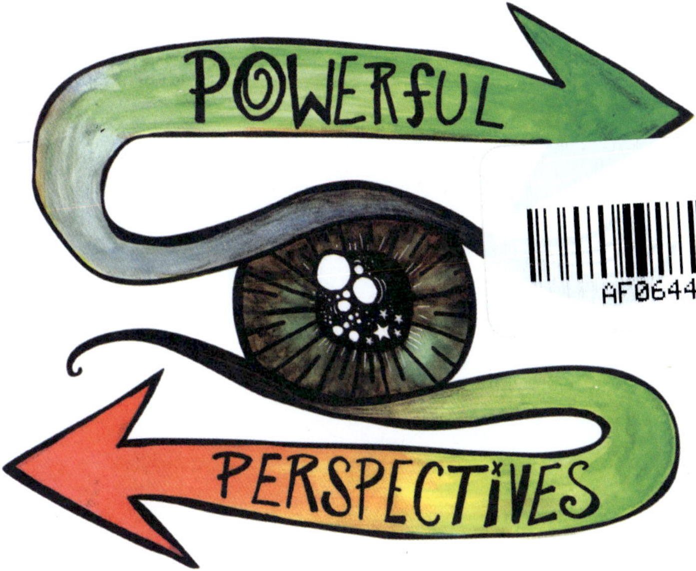

POWERFUL PERSPECTIVES

An Oracle Deck

REDFeather
MIND | BODY | SPIRIT
4880 Lower Valley Road, Atglen, PA 19310

Words by Amanda Rhodes
Art by AmyChace

Copyright © 2022 by Amanda Rhodes and Amy Chace

Library of Congress Control Number: 2022932682

All rights reserved. No part of this work may be reproduced or used in any form or by any means—graphic, electronic, or mechanical, including photocopying or information storage and retrieval systems—without written permission from the publisher.

The scanning, uploading, and distribution of this book or any part thereof via the Internet or any other means without the permission of the publisher is illegal and punishable by law. Please purchase only authorized editions and do not participate in or encourage the electronic piracy of copyrighted materials.

"Red Feather Mind Body Spirit" logo is a trademark of Schiffer Publishing, Ltd.

"Red Feather Mind Body Spirit Feather" logo is a registered trademark of Schiffer Publishing, Ltd.

Designed by Danielle D. Farmer
Cover design by Danielle D. Farmer
Type set in Segoe Script/Tomarik/Avenir

ISBN: 978-0-7643-6522-5
Printed in China

Published by REDFeather Mind, Body, Spirit
An imprint of Schiffer Publishing, Ltd.

4880 Lower Valley Road
Atglen, PA 19310
Phone: (610) 593-1777; Fax: (610) 593-2002
Email: Info@redfeathermbs.com
Web: www.redfeathermbs.com

For our complete selection of fine books on this and related subjects, please visit our website at www.redfeathermbs.com. You may also write for a free catalog.

I dedicate this deck to all those who made a safe space for me to pursue art. That list includes (but is not limited to) my parents (Sharon and Ernie), my husband (Paul), and Ron Kelleher, my high school art teacher. Ron not only made a safe space to make art, he encouraged me and also recognized me when I didn't even know I needed it. He saw me. Thank you to all for all!

xoxoxo, Amy

This work is dedicated to my friend Andrea Piotrowski. Without you, I may never have walked through this door and would have missed out on so many amazing things. Thank you for your friendship, your support, and your unwavering belief in me and my journey.

A huge thank you to Reflections Books for your support and providing me a safe and beautiful space to work. Thank you to all of my clients near and far who inspire me and allow me to do this amazing work.

Of course I also dedicate this work to my family, but mainly my beautiful son, Ian, who was my catalyst to start exploring my spirituality and to realign with my divine connection to Spirit.

—Amanda

A Note from Amy
(the Artist)

This deck is called *Powerful Perspectives* for an important reason. I created the artwork specifically so it can be viewed, enjoyed, and interpreted from more than one angle or perspective. So many things in life should be viewed from a variety of angles, so why not imagery? These cards technically do not have reversals. The companion book uses the word "reversals" simply for ease of use, but have no fear—these are not your customary Tarot reversals. Each perspective has a meaning all its own. No perspective is taking anything away from you. Each perspective is only adding to the possibilities.

A Note from Amanda
(the Author)

Powerful Perspectives is an oracle deck like none I have ever seen before (and trust me, I own an embarrassing number of decks). I have written the companion book by using my interpretations of the symbols and the feelings I get from the beautiful images on the cards, but I want you to use your intuition. We have left so much room untouched so that you can give each card your own unique spin and meaning. I hope this deck will become part of your main rotation for daily guidance and inspiration. Sometimes all we need to go from a place of disempowerment to empowerment is a new perspective. Your power is in the now. You get to choose how you look at things and whether you see obstacles or opportunities. Choose wisely and well always.

Contents

Introduction........................8		
How to Use This Deck...........9		
Card Descriptions................10		

Card 1 11	Card 15 44	Card 29 72
Card 2 13	Card 16 46	Card 30 74
Card 3 15	Card 17 48	Card 31 76
Card 4 17	Card 18 50	Card 32 78
Card 5 20	Card 19 52	Card 33 80
Card 6 23	Card 20 54	Card 34 82
Card 7 26	Card 21 56	Card 35 84
Card 8 28	Card 22 58	Card 36 86
Card 9 30	Card 23 60	Card 37 88
Card 10 33	Card 24 62	Card 38 90
Card 11 35	Card 25 64	Card 39 92
Card 12 37	Card 26 66	Card 40 94
Card 13 39	Card 27 68	
Card 14 41	Card 28 70	

Conclusion........................96

Introduction

Welcome to *Powerful Perspectives*! We are so glad that you have been drawn to choose this deck. Whether you're doing a one-card pull to set intentions for your day, doing a three-card spread, or pulling as many cards as you like, we hope that this deck will serve you and grow with you over time. You can use our interpretation of the cards, but there have been so many symbols left for your individual perspective. You will never see this deck the same way twice, thanks to the depth of the artwork and the multitude of symbols depicted on each card. Go ahead and look at the cards sideways if you like, and feel free to have fun and ascribe your own meanings. Intuition should always be a fun and creative process!

How to Use This Deck

Whether you are a longtime user of divinatory tools or this is your first oracle deck (be careful—decks are addictive!), a good first step is to go through the deck and touch each card. Look at the images and feel the vibration of your deck. Once you've gone through the cards, hold them against your heart and set your intention for the deck. I usually use something like this: "I pray that the insight given by these cards will always be timely, true, and helpful."

When you're ready to use them, take a deep breath to ground your energy, think of the question or situation you have in mind, and shuffle the cards. If you have any cards that automatically fall out, these are called "jumpers." Make sure you pay particular attention to them since that is the universe's way of ensuring you get the right card in the right moment, although the cards that come out of the deck are never an accident, no matter how you choose to draw them. You can shuffle them mindfully or throw them on the ground fifty-two-pickup style. You'll always get the right cards for your situation.

Whether you draw one card to set daily intentions, or three cards for a more in-depth look at a situation, there are no rules!

We hope that these cards will continue to be a trusted friend and guide as you move throughout your life.

Card Descriptions

CARD 1

UPRIGHT

Inner self-awakening, making choices, silencing the noise and the expectations of other people when it comes to living in alignment with the true self. Old wisdom bursting forward. Looking for clarity, achieving quiet.

Things are changing and your inner wisdom is stirring. You are noticing more and more things around you that are creating noise and chaos, and you are feeling the pull of wanting to come home to your inner self. Now is the time to allow that inner self to speak and pull you in new directions, even when it feels illogical. Old beliefs/stories/situations/people/relationships are falling away, and you are completely equipped to handle the changes that are being presented. It's time for clear boundaries, allowing yourself to hear the birdsong and the music on the wind, letting everyone else's expectations be carried away. You blossom in the most beautiful way when you silence the noise, come home to who you really are, and trust in your own wisdom.

REVERSAL

Resistance, hanging on to things that no longer serve you out of fear of the unknown. Reluctance to leap. Growth occurring when the leap is taken, self-assuredness and confidence on the steps forward. Why are you hanging on and what are you unwilling to release?

It's time to take the leap! As the wisdom of your soul takes the first leap, you hesitate, digging your fingernails into the way things have been, although you know that they are no longer serving you. What are you holding on to and what are you fearing in this moment? Is the fear of the unknown as large as you imagine? There is always going to be fear of failure, and there is never a perfect moment to make the leap, but you are being called to grow. If you fall on your face, so what? You get up, you dust yourself off, you honor yourself for the amazing risk taker you are, and you rise up stronger and more resilient than ever before. It's time to see your true potential, cut the anchors away that hold you back, and take a leap of faith. Spirit will be there to cushion your landing on sunnier shores.

UPRIGHT

Resting in knowledge of protection and spiritual support. Creativity and intuition peaking, there is more than is being presented. Allowing the universe to unfold before you.

You are not responsible for knowing it all or doing it all. Spirit is encouraging you to rest and to know that this rest is required to allow new insights to emerge. It is safe to stop. Know that you are receiving guidance and information even when you feel like you are not making any outward effort to do so. When we can fully release ourselves from our earthbound existence and constant striving, we are free to return to our true nature as infinite beings and receive higher guidance. Your "Spirit Posse" (guides, guardians, archangels, ascended masters, and loved ones) is watching over you and putting the required pieces in place. Immense knowledge is being made available to you at this time through synchronicity and serendipitous events. You are exactly where you need to be, and you are safe. Achieve more by doing less. Know that it is all being taken care of and that you are looked after by Spirit. All things are possible. Make time for meditation, relaxation, and self-care.

REVERSAL

Cyclops with eye closed (one eye, one perspective), flinging love outward, love coming from head, mouth covered, unable to express love, unable to see true potential, unable to see opportunity for creativity.

There is more to life than what is presented directly in front of you. Open your eyes, take a deeper look, and be open to new perspectives. Try not to get so fixated on one thing that you end up missing everything else that is going on around you. Open your eyes to love and you open your eyes to miracles. At the core of your being, you are love. Love flows to you and through you in a beautiful energetic exchange with the universe. Through love, all things are created, and the world needs your unique point of view at this time. Speak up and be open to new perspectives. Once you start seeing the light of the truth and speaking authentically from your heart and soul, doors open for you. New opportunities abound as soon as you open up to receive.

CARD 3

UPRIGHT

Gallery, jury, judgment. Nighttime, shadow, dark work, feeling intense emotion, processing information, the light will come again. Infinite potential, intention setting, doing new things without expectation, ghosts of the past, "if at first you don't succeed, try, try again."

You are being asked to release the past and come back into the present. You can be your own worst critic, and it may feel like the weight of the world is pressing on you at this time. A million eyes are watching, and you are afraid that you might trip up or drop one of the million balls you seem to be juggling right now. This might be a time of taking on too much and the ego not wanting to admit that some prioritizing needs to be done. It is good to give, and good to care about others in the spirit of service and wanting to help, but at this point it is detrimental for you to do so. Too much has been taken on. Gracefully bow out of anything that does not absolutely need to be done, before you implode.

REVERSAL

Confusion, balance between earth realm and universal realm, finding your feet again, Spirit is righting you, finding your feet, clearing the fog. Hidden rainbows, good fortune

Things are a little confusing at the moment. You are being asked to come down and ground your energy. It's hard to plot the way forward when there is energy flying in all directions and you can't seem to focus on one opportunity. This feeling will pass when you make room for conscious connection with Spirit. Make time to send your roots down into the earth, and allow the earth to nourish and support you. Quiet the chatter that is going on so you can hear the whispered wisdom that is all around you. Spirit is working to bring clarity and to help you place your feet firmly back on the ground so that you may focus and stand in truth. Feel the breath coming in and out of your lungs. Know that you are supported, nurtured, and safe.

CARD 4

UPRIGHT

Cups overflowing, emotional fulfillment, opportunity, intention manifesting, abundance, prosperity, messages of good fortune, babies, marriages, relationship harmony, contentment

This is a time of prosperity, and you are really owning your excellence. You are seeing yourself as the embodiment of Spirit. It's awesome that you are experiencing your dreams coming to life all around you. There's a glow about you, and you are acting as a magnet, attracting your wildest dreams. Trust that your cups are running over and that this is a time of joy. Don't forget to share the wealth and bounty with others. You are inspiring them to trust in the universe as well! You know that all of your needs will always be met, and you are celebrating your joy and success. This is a time of good news when it comes to new jobs, new homes, marriages, babies, engagements—the list goes on!

There are so many wonderful reasons to celebrate. Straighten your crown, my friend. You have worked hard to get all of this abundance, so accept any accolades that come your way. Yes, it's a good thing to be humble, but at other times you need to shake your booty with wild abandon as you dance around your living room. Now is that time! You're in a good place and you have the Midas touch. Relationships are harmonious as you support others and you are supported. The love is being exchanged both ways, and the channel is wide and open. Enjoy this time!

REVERSAL

Ideas are springing forward from the ether into your head. There are parrots in the room. Would you want what you say repeated? Keep cards close to your chest, amplification of intention, what goes around comes around!

You are being encouraged to speak consciously, and remember that not everyone has your best interest at heart all the time. It's a good time to check in with your intuition and see if everything really is as it appears to be. If you wouldn't put it on a T-shirt, it's not the best thing to be saying out loud in mixed company. There are also people who are repeating what you say, so keep your integrity and that stellar reputation you have at the top of your mind. It doesn't matter what they say anyway. All that matters is your perception of yourself and your reasons for doing what you are doing. If you are making plans for a new project or business venture, be discerning about where you share this information. Your intuition is on fire, so trust what you hear and see when it comes to people and situations. If it seems too good to be true, it likely *is* too good to be true. You want to see the best in everyone, and we understand that. Be your best, stand in integrity, and show that shining, beautiful self everywhere you go, secure in who you are and who you are becoming.

CARD  5

UPRIGHT

Seeing with new eyes, more than things appear to be, notice the little things, the wisdom in creating one's own reality, getting closer to spirit, higher vibration, small rewards vs. big ones

Watch me pull some awesome out of my hat. It looks like a feather or a flower, but it is so much more. This is your intention being made manifest in your life, and you have the ability to see relationships, situations, and objects with new eyes. Sometimes it isn't about reaping the big rewards; it's about seeing the smaller steps that are getting you to those big goals, and that hard work you are putting in is being noticed. When you take the time to pay attention to detail and do your work honestly, it is noticed. This could indicate that your energy is going to shift. Things are going to speed up and doors are opening. Opportunities abound and are coming at you full force. You're excited, focused, and aligned. As your vibration increases, you cocreate hand in hand with the universe. Some people might think you have your head in the clouds, but that couldn't be further from the truth. You are grounded and creating with beautiful and deliberate intention, using all the wisdom that has brought you to this point. You are absolutely on the right track here, and you are receiving indications of that truth everywhere you turn. Look for the small things, since they are the trail markers to the big victories. Stay focused. See clearly.

REVERSAL

Cat, three hearts, snowman, ending of winter, Mona Lisa smile, self-assured, standing firm in your own power, inner knowing, feeling solid, making plans, keeping your own counsel, three principles—love, trust, understanding. Giving these to yourself first rather than to others. Learning who you are in your own process of evolution.

Just like the Mona Lisa, your heart wears a smile, and you're the only one who knows exactly why. Is it that you are smiling at the person looking at you, or is it the satisfaction of having a plan underway? This is the end of a period where you have felt lost or fogged in. The ice is melting and you are getting ready to spring forward into new plans and opportunities. These ideas have been brewing under the surface for some time, and they are the key to your independence. It's time to keep your own counsel and stay true to your desires. This is a time of love, trust, understanding, and being safe in your own skin. Life is becoming vibrant and beautiful as you let go of any preconceived notions of the way things "should" be, whether those notions belong to you or whether those notions are imposed upon you by other people in your life. There's a beauty to being independent and confident in who you are. You are in that space now, and you don't have to tell anyone about the secret behind your smile if you choose not to. You are evolving and you are setting yourself free.

CARD 6

UPRIGHT

Questioning, doubting, wondering, looking to the heavens for answers, illusion falling away, dark night of the soul, dawn is coming.

Do you hear that chime? That's the call of Spirit. You know that there is more to this world than what is presented, and you may have been spending some time questioning this lately. If you've been hearing things, feeling things, or being woken in the night, this is your time of spiritual awakening. Spirit is calling to you to look to the heavens and to see the connection that has been with you all along. You are supported. Lately it may not feel that way, but when you look and ask for help, you will receive the answer. Be aware that this help comes in a myriad of ways. It could just be a random thought coming into your head, or unsolicited advice coming from a stranger. Now is the time to truly awaken and look at ways that you can use that intuitive knowledge. The time for sleeping is over. It's time to take action. This could mean you are stepping more into alignment with your purpose, while knowing that it is not necessary for you to do this alone. Seek an expert or a mentor, or take a look at some possibilities when it comes to education and furthering your knowledge. The light is beckoning in the darkness. Walk toward it and embrace your true potential.

REVERSAL

You are made of the stuff of stars, expansion, rest. You don't have to push so hard to grow. Decrease commitments, overwhelm, seek balance between the realms.

You are the universe and the universe is you. Make time for conscious connection, knowing that you are safe and supported. Make sure that you are not contributing to your own detriment and that you are making time to care for yourself in whatever way you feel is needed at this time. Put your feet in the grass and connect to the heavens and the earth. Feel their energy flowing through your entire being, and know that you are connected to both realms. We live balanced between the earth and the heavens. When we are too earth centered, we become more focused on material things and tend to worry quite a bit. When we are too centered in the universe, we get so caught up in looking ahead and trying to see the future that we miss what is in front of us. We commit without taking time to check in and find out whether we are actually capable of doing what we promised. Allow yourself to see clearly and to be honest with your commitments, while making time to seek balance. You already know which areas of your life need to be tweaked and rebalanced, so take appropriate steps to do so. There's no rush. Breathe, be, trust, and allow. You don't always have to push so hard to grow. It happens organically on its own. Stop fighting the current.

CARD

UPRIGHT

Owning your awesome, things coming into alignment, living in full expression, self-actualization, being a beacon and role model for others, living unapologetically, ease and flow

This is a time where things are coming into alignment and you are beginning to see that your efforts to manifest your best life are paying off. It's likely that you've had to make some difficult decisions, to release people and situations, and that the process has been messy. Now you can really fly. You've made sacrifices and defined your boundaries as you've stepped into universal flow. You are empowering others to do the same. It's time to notice the ease in which your life unfolds when you are not fighting against the current of the universe. You are realizing that you are a magnificent being, worthy of living your best life. Nothing can hold you back. Expect others to approach you and ask how you got to this place of complete self-assurance. Shrug your shoulders and give them a wink. Just kidding! Open your heart. It is safe to talk to others openly. It's you they want to hear from, not everyone else's *idea* of who you should be, but you—unfiltered, open, and honest.

REVERSAL

Hiding the self, not revealing truth, pleasing others, duality, two lives, reconciling duality, allowing love to burst forth

The saying goes that the eyes are the window to the soul, but yours are covered. Why is this? Whether it is hiding for the sake of keeping up appearances, or to appease other people's expectations, or you are worried that you will not be accepted for who you are, you need to know that your true essence is oozing out, and you won't be able to hold it back forever. You deserve to be who you are, unashamed and unapologetic. What have you been hiding? There are places in your life right now that are not aligned with Spirit. I used to live like this when I was in the "psychic closet," terrified to tell people who or what I was. The best decision I ever made was coming out and living in alignment with who I am. Even if you don't come jumping out of the closet with both feet, let yourself be seen as much as you are comfortable. This unfolding and blossoming can be a gradual process. In any event, this unfolding belongs to you. Love yourself in your unfolding. Don't seek external validation. Put yourself first.

CARD 8

UPRIGHT

Calm, quiet, contemplative, finding a safe space to speak, unburdening the self, listening, understanding, trusting the process, a time of stillness, reflection, releasing

You may be feeling as though life's pace has really slowed down, and it's frustrating not making the progress that you feel you should be making. There's a lot going on, and you have been burdened with the energy of others and feeling overwhelmed. Unfortunately, not being a burden of the physical kind, the way to put down what you're carrying is to find a safe space and a safe person to listen. Whether that's a real person, a pet, a loved one on the other side, or pouring your heart out to a journal or to Spirit in general, pull up a chair and start releasing these burdens. There is a lot that needs to be processed. Spirit wants you to know that you are always supported and guided and that tender space in your heart is being filled with love, trust, and compassion.

Feel the energy of the earth and the universe supporting you. Ground yourself, be free, and release your burdens so you can move forward.

REVERSAL

Increasing energy, blossoming, new ideas, new opportunities, faster energetic pace

You are emerging from a time of quiet and rest, and you are full to the brim with new ideas. It's time to take action, but you have so many ideas and choices that you aren't sure where to go. Use your intuition like a divining rod. Prioritize according to which options feel best to you. Like a tree, each branch has more branches that come from it, so there are many forks in the road and many adventures possible. Revel in the excitement that comes from this energy of potential. Jump out of your comfort zone. You are worthy of the best at any given moment. It's not once you achieve something or get something, you are worthy now. The sum of your experiences and the willingness to let yourself go through a period of rest have replenished your energy. Trust that you have the knowledge to get where you need to go. You are blossoming, and everything you are touching at this time is being nourished and nurtured in the right way. Take action and watch how quickly the pace of life ramps up. Spirit is celebrating and so should you! Do a dance like nobody's watching (who cares if they are?!) and take the first step!

CARD 9

UPRIGHT

Contemplation, how to be of service, realign with purpose, help others, listening to the beat of your heart, making room for spirit, completion, alignment, steps, levels

Do you hear that drumming within you? Your heartbeat is your primal connection to your soul. The blood is thrumming through your ears, pushed by that beautiful and vibrant heart. As you wake up in the morning, ask yourself how you may best serve others and yourself. Lift yourself as well as others, and be open and receptive. What's happening right now is not currently feeding that need for fulfillment. Ask your soul what you need. Your needs are important too. What can bring you back into alignment with Spirit? Small changes can make a big difference. Follow the beat of your heart to the places within yourself. Make room for quiet connection and direction from Spirit on your next steps. Look to the stars and follow what is important to you. You are being pulled and driven to make changes. You do not have to know all the answers. As you pursue what you are passionate about, the drumbeat will pick up and you will start running straight into your destiny. Celebrate taking your first steps on the next leg of your journey.

REVERSAL

Heightened intuition, awakening, illusions dropping, seeing clearly, signs, guideposts, warnings, seeing all perspectives

You are being called to awaken at this time. You might find that you are actually physically being awakened in the night. You are asked to open your third-eye chakra, which allows you to see things as they really are. Sometimes this means that we need to see things without emotion involved. I know it seems counterintuitive to tell you to take emotions out of what you are seeing right now. Our emotions are our internal guidance system, but we need to allow ourselves to see our current circumstances more clearly. It's easy to justify our circumstances by using our emotions. Maybe that person didn't mean to hurt us, maybe we are off-track because we are meant to be, or maybe Spirit puts little buoys in the way to center and direct us or warn us of obstacles that are unseen at this time. Look deeply with your eye of truth, and trust what is being received. As you see more clearly, illusions fall away and you see things as they are. Navigate by the stars and by the beating of your heart. Heed any warnings that are heard at this time, and expect signs from Spirit that guide you on your way. Signs come in so many shapes and forms. It could be a conversation, a billboard you see, something you read, lights flickering on or off, or gut feelings. Trust what you are receiving.

CARD 10

UPRIGHT

Embarrassment, feeling alone, know support is all around you, ask for help, listen to the advice you receive with your heart, emotional wounding/healing

Whether you have given your trust or your vulnerability to someone who took advantage of it, or whether you have overcommitted yourself, you need to know that it is okay to ask for help. You may feel embarrassed about taking on too much. It's okay; your enthusiasm is a trait that you should be proud of. Remember the support all around you and know that nobody is going to look at you and say, "I told you so." Look and listen with your heart, knowing that you will be guided to the right helpers for you. You are not meant to know it all, and there is growth in this process. Reach out and someone will help you up. Relieve yourself of heavy feelings. You will eventually see the beauty in this moment even though it is not obvious now. Allow yourself to receive love and support from others, and really look at the solutions that are being offered. Your way is not the only way to get things done. You'd be surprised what you hear when you open your heart and your mind to listen. You are never making a fool of yourself by asking for help when you need it, and you never need to suffer in silence. Open up where you feel safe to do so, and receive the healing love from the ones the universe has chosen to help you.

REVERSAL

Chasing miracles? Rely on your guides, give it to the universe. Miracles occur when you relax. See the divinity in the self. Cocreation.

Are you spending time chasing the divine? You are a seeker, and you are looking everywhere for the miracles every New Age author tells you exist. Maybe you meditate for hours on end after ascending a mountaintop. Perhaps you visit a far-off temple. My dear, you could have saved yourself the journey, since the divinity is in yourself. It's been there the whole time in the light in your eyes and the beating of your heart. It's in your interactions with others and the life that you are creating. Things come into alignment when you recognize yourself as the beautiful, multifaceted being that you are. When you realize that you are the divine, it's easier to treat yourself with the love that you deserve. I assure you that the only person who is hard on you is you, and the only competition against you is the competition you create. Allow yourself to breathe fully, your shoulders to drop, and everything to unclench. You ARE divine. Stop searching and know that you too are wearing a beautiful halo of light. Be gentle and kind to yourself. You're on the right track. Don't create resistance. Live with ease.

UPRIGHT

Energy and intuition heighten, new jobs, new businesses, inventions, ideas, widening awareness of the earth and the heavens, spirit downloads, ideas, celebration

You don't need coffee to get yourself going right now. Expect a surge in energy and creativity. Do what inspires you. Write down your ideas, write to-do lists, and keep yourself motivated, because your brain is growing vast forests of ideas. Each idea is leading to another, so now is a fantastic time to start pursuing the new paths. This could also indicate you are thinking about changing up your career and looking for a new job if the old one hasn't been fulfilling you in the ways that it used to. There's no point in wasting time; you're on fire and your ideas are great. Carry a notebook or a digital recorder to capture those ideas. Your mind is being opened to new possibilities and awareness of the earth and the heavens. Ride this wave of creativity and allow it to flow through you. You are birthing beautiful new conditions and ideas. Been thinking of starting up your own business or inventing something new? Now is a time of inspired action. Enjoy, explore, and celebrate your boundless creativity.

REVERSAL

Stop, listen, regroup. Preconceived notions, what stories do you want to change? Looking at yourself and others from a new angle. Reinvention.

If you could pull yourself up out of your body and look down on yourself, what would you see? What assumptions and judgments are you making about yourself? Go get a piece of paper and write those things down. What are those stories and where have they come from? You may be feeling some confusion around who you are at this time. This is a time of reinvention. The ideas you are putting into motion right now will result in success. It's understandable that this can be a confusing time. You are standing at a crossroads, and it's time to work on the relationship you have with yourself. Close the eye of logic and dream big. Allow your heart to create the next iteration of you. Look from a different angle or perspective. What needs changing, what needs fixing, and what is absolutely brilliant? Don't forget to see the wonderful parts of yourself that already shine for all to see. Stop, regroup, and get clear on where you are going!

CARD 12

UPRIGHT

Beauty is in the eye of the beholder, your power is in your perception, what is repeating? Self-examination, releasing what doesn't resonate with who you are becoming. Stay away from gossip and other people's drama; it usually ends in heartache. What do you want in your world? You have the power to make it happen!

Your universe is in the way you are beholding it. What are you seeing? What are you choosing to see? Your power is in your perspective. Your cup is full of emotion, and your head is full of dreams that are longing to take wing and flourish. Remember that no matter where you are in life, whether you feel lost or like something is missing, you are whole. Make your own decisions at this time. Look honestly and see where patterns are repeating and where beliefs and actions need to be changed or released. Your thoughts and beliefs create the universe you see. If your thoughts or beliefs don't fit in your vision of the world you want to create, let them go. Make space for only your best. You are the king or queen of your own perception, just and true.

Create a world where you can be free to spread your wings and fly.

REVERSAL

Building, acceleration, job advancement, moving onto the next steps, evolution, people want to know the key to your success, making a wish, seeing the full picture, not getting too caught up in your own success, remaining humble, ease, fear of success

Your intentions, dedication, and hard work have brought you to where you are, and you need to know that it is being noticed. It's not only being noticed by the people whom you might happen to work for, but by other people in your circle who want to know what the secret is to your success. You can be honest with them. It was intention put into action with blood, sweat, and tears. You might be feeling some insecurity at this point, that if you stop working as hard that all of this is going to disappear. Spirit wants to remind you that you receive what you put out there, and the fear of falling backward is not something that you want to project. Allow yourself to rest here for a moment so that you can set the next steps into motion. This could mean that you will be going up a rung on the corporate ladder, or that new opportunities are coming your way when it comes to employment or finance. Expect a bump in your earnings. Your success belongs to you and no one else. There have been no shortcuts. You deserve all the accolades that are being received right now. Keep your humility about you and keep a cool head. Make sure that you are looking at the whole picture and that you are aware of what you are getting yourself into. Take time to think and digest information. Check in with your spirit. It's worked for you well so far!

CARD 13

UPRIGHT

Black and white, blah, apathy, stuck, everyone else moving forward, why not me? Cheering gecko thinks you can do it! Finding your groove, self-care, motivation, make a list, break down those goals, bring color into your space, seek beauty and blessings.

It's hard when you feel stuck on the sidelines, especially when it appears everyone else is advancing at the speed of light. They know what they want, and they're going for it. Good for them, right? Sometimes when we look really hard, we miss the main point. It's not about achieving all of life's goals in line with your ten-year plan. Who really has one of those, anyway? Most people are simply flying by the seat of their pants most of the time, despite what it looks like on social media. Make changes. Find your flavor. Find what excites you. Journal and make a list, writing down the things that really light your fire and get you excited. Start following those bread crumbs. Begin to notice the blessings that are all around you. Take care of yourself in the best way you know how. Break things down into smaller goals if you are feeling overwhelmed, and take one small step today that's going to change events unfolding in your life. Are you rolling your eyes at this card description and thinking that it's easy for us to say? We think you can do it, and if you look at the bottom left of this card you'll see a cheering gecko who knows you can do it too. This funk will not last forever!

REVERSAL

Looking back, changing perception, seeing your growth, noticing your individuality, seeing yourself for the divine being that you are, looking at self with love rather than criticism. What's your "why"? Are you doing what you're doing for approval or because it lights you up and fulfills you?

You are able to look at yourself with love and know that the actions that took place in the past are not what defines your future. You are realizing that the choices you have made have had their part in molding who you are, allowing you to embrace the you that resides in the now. You know that you no longer have to hold on to any of those old burdens. You can rest in the awareness that just as you are doing your best now, you were doing your best then. Look upon yourself with compassion. Look on others with the same compassion that you give yourself. See with clear eyes and use curiosity rather than judgment in your interactions with others. You should be pleased with the growth you have achieved. You are ready to be comfortable in your own skin, living on your terms rather than seeking approval from others.

It is safe for you to speak your truth, and it is necessary at this time.

Walk away from these conversations with a lighter heart, knowing that in letting the truth flow free, you have given yourself permission to release and relax any tension that has made itself at home within you. You have done what's right by speaking up for yourself and others, and that's what really matters. The hidden gift within these conversations is an opportunity to open up a dialogue where none existed, opening gateways to better communication and understanding.

REVERSAL

Time for the parade, coming out of the closet with how you really feel, showing off your true self, people are talking about you and wondering where you've been, social engagements, people want to share your energy and be around you, you want to be around people, have a good time.

It's time to get outside and socialize. You've been indoors too long, and you are ready to get out and about. Your friends have been looking for you, and it's likely you have had a few missed calls. Time to get out there and strut your stuff. If you haven't had friends looking for you, then now is a great time to get out there and forge new friendships. Your social calendar is going to be revving up, so take advantage of this energy and have fun. Remember that your vibe attracts your tribe, so get ready to meet new friends, friends of friends, and potential romantic relationships. If you are already in a relationship, you've probably been thinking about moving things to the next level. A little birdie is here to tell you that you are ready to move it on up to the next level. Enjoy this fun and fast-paced time. Let your hair down. Let people see the real and true you and you will attract people just like a magnet. Others are attracted to the vibrant energy that's surrounding you at this time. You do you and the rest will take care of itself.

CARD 15

UPRIGHT

Planning, industriousness, saving for lean times, thinking ahead, working hard, don't forget to play now and then, running around without purpose or running around and not getting much accomplished, paying attention to dreams, intuition, journaling

Your brain is full of new ideas, and you have so much you want to do that it's hard to focus. Spirit wants you to make a plan and think things through. Sometimes we get so excited that we just start running around wasting time and getting nothing accomplished. It's a lot easier to get things done when you put a plan into action. Break things up into realistic and doable steps and start there. You can always build one idea off the next. Think things through. I feel like I need to say that twice. You may want to be putting resources away as you start to consider putting this plan into action. You could be finding an increase in dream communication. Pay attention to these, and keep a journal beside your bed for the purpose of writing these insights down. They may not make sense to you now, but they will become clear once you sit with them a while. Pull yourself away from the television or your devices and make time for journaling every day so that you can empty out some of those brilliant ideas that are bouncing around in your head. Seeing everything on paper may help you when it comes to sorting through it all and prioritizing and planning your next steps. Get as clear as you can on your way forward, while keeping in mind that the way you think it should go is not the only way it can go. Be open to detours along the way.

REVERSAL

Dreaming of possibilities, being pushed by Spirit, guided, writing, channeled writing, developing intuition, "a-ha" moments

There are so many possibilities in front of you, and you may find yourself overwhelmed by it all. The angel on your shoulder is asking you to come back to the now. It's time to check in with yourself. Do some grounding and bring yourself back to earth. Your hopes and dreams will blossom, but it all depends on the seeds you plant and nurture now. You are finding yourself looking for guidance, so try grabbing your journal, asking for the guidance you desire, and write down whatever comes in. You might be surprised at your own insight or the messages that appear when you aren't "trying" so hard to find all the answers. Relax at ease in the now. Gather your strength. When things start moving, they'll move quickly.

CARD 16

UPRIGHT

Standing up, independence, seeing the bigger picture. Facing conflict/obstacles/opposition with confidence and authenticity. Remembering not to create resistance, be true to yourself, the world needs your unique perspective. Know that you see things as they are.

It's time to stand up for what you believe is right, even when you are coming chest to chest with challenge and opposition. This is not to resist other points of view or to convince others to come to your viewpoint, but for your own integrity. It's time to walk your talk. The bigger picture is different for everyone, since we are all walking different paths, but it's time to be true to you. Remember that it's better to fight *for* something than *against* another thing. When we push against, we actually perpetuate that which we don't want. Remember, what you put your focus on expands. You can move forward with confidence and authenticity when you are in alignment with Spirit. People can give you as much side-eye as they want, but don't let that deter you. You are seeing the big picture, and the world needs your unique point of view.

REVERSAL

Listening with heart rather than ears, singing your own song, moving by instinct, emotions being released and brought to the surface, allowing time for processing and release, walking your own path, go with the flow.

Listen fully. When you listen with your heart rather than your ears alone, you will be better able to separate truth from illusion. Listen to the music of your soul or any music that really uplifts you. It's time to reach higher heights as Spirit is pushing you forward. You are advancing with ease and moving in line with your instincts right now. Feel the way forward. Stop looking so hard for the answers. The answers aren't really "answers" anyway. Life is in constant flux and flow, so follow the current and go with the flow as you sing your own song, forge your own path, and find your own answers. Emotions are bound to bubble up to the surface when you make time to listen to the very depths of your soul. This is a good thing. Process these emotions and allow them to be expressed.

CARD 17

UPRIGHT

Reconciling dual nature, hiding part of yourself, fertility, new ideas bursting forward, making plans on the down-low and bringing them to light, sharing your ideas.

You've been in the quiet planning stages of taking the leap and doing something new. It might even feel like you have been living a bit of a double life as you prepare to shed an old skin and step fully into the next phase of your life. Until now, these have just been dreams, and you may not have bared your soul and shared your plans with the people around you, out of fears of apathy or not being supported by the people in your life. This is a fertile time for creation, and you are bursting with excitement for what is to come. It's time to start talking about these new plans, knowing that you will be supported. You might be surprised to find that there's more support than you thought there would be. Put your cards on the table; it's time to make your intentions known and start taking action!

REVERSAL

Getting pulled into drama, don't enable, delegate where possible. Use mature judgment and diplomacy. This could be a touchy situation!

Get your goggles—there's a drama storm coming. You might find yourself going through a time of unexpected challenges, but don't worry; these are for the better! Try to keep yourself separate from becoming a peacemaker or mediator. People in your life are looking to you to sort out their problems, and you might just end up holding the big pile of work that needs to be done. The trouble is that the willing horse often gets the load, and you have the strength, reliability, and skills to sort everything out. Keep a calm demeanor and use mature judgment and diplomacy. Try not to allow yourself to get pulled right into the thick of things. Keep a higher perspective and delegate where possible. Unfortunately, the people around you will not learn to keep things in balance if you are constantly stepping in and doing it for them. Help where needed, but don't do all the heavy lifting.

CARD 18

UPRIGHT

Rebirth, reflection on the paths you've followed, a time of reevaluating priorities or making decisions, possibility, responsibility, revisiting lessons learned

A cycle is coming to completion, and it's time to reflect and look back on the paths that you have traveled, the lessons that have been learned, and the priorities that have changed. It's time for an honest reflection of circumstances as they are currently, and making plans for the way forward. What would you like to accomplish now? Your power is in your hands as you step into a new cycle. Everything has a time and a place, an ebb and a flow, and time stands still for no one. Eyes are on you as those who are in your circle watch to see what you'll do, and look forward to celebrating your success with you. Rejoice in the lessons you have learned and see how far you've come. Celebrate yourself. Do something that is just for you, and enjoy this beautiful time of reflection and self-love. You're pretty spectacular!

REVERSAL

Family relationships, feeling out of alignment with source, a need to awaken, how are you nourishing yourself and your soul?

You're busy but you're being asked to put your focus back on home and family. The people who are closest to you are starting to miss you. You have a lot of priorities and a lot of things to do, but these people will not always be around. Take time to build relationships with your family now, whether that be your chosen family or your biological one. Coming back to your roots and simpler times will bring your feet back to the ground. You're running around so fast, they barely touch the earth. Nourish yourself with the love of your family, your tribe, or the people who matter most. The rest can wait as you bring yourself back down to earth, rest, and reawaken stronger than ever before. Make time for meditation and reflection so that you can take time for yourself and recharge. There's no need to go, go, go.

CARD 19

UPRIGHT

Go for it! Spread your light everywhere, inspire, uplift, empower, social conventions, expectations of others, established structures, breaking the mold.

Throw your hands in the air and spread your light like you legitimately care! It could make people around you uncomfortable, but who cares? You are feeling energy coursing through you, and the need to express yourself fully. People may laugh, roll their eyes, or call you crazy, but you're really inspiring them to live in alignment with their joy as well. Sure, we can live in line with the expectations that other people place on us, we can follow the prescribed path, but is that living? Know that you are stepping into a leadership role as you follow your bliss and fill your heart with love. You get one life; what are you choosing to do with it? Throw caution to the wind and really live! Now is the time to go for it. Have fun, get dirty, and make mistakes, then dust yourself off and do it again! Cut loose and have fun.

REVERSAL

Sitting in suspended animation; knowledge to move forward and loosen the bonds that you have placed on yourself; being supported by your wisdom, guides, guardians; receiving divine love

Feeling stuck or like nothing's moving forward? Could it be possible that you are forgetting that you have the knowledge and wisdom to release yourself from this funky feeling of being out of control? You are never stuck. There are always options, but you could be choosing not to see them or not to make a move at this time. More information is needed before you proceed. Know that your guides and guardians have your back and are helping to bring you back on track. Some of the limitations that you are putting on circumstances and your own progress are self-imposed. Yeah, we know that nobody likes to hear that, but when you look at your own attitudes and judgment toward your own forward movement, pay particular attention to the excuses (ahem . . . I mean *reasons*) that you are bringing up to block your own progress. See yourself and your magnificence in the way that you are seen by the universe. You have unlimited potential. Know that you can move forward with ease once you examine and remove the limits you have imposed on yourself.

UPRIGHT

Good fortune, opportunity, protection, calm water, dreams manifesting, thistle, aggressiveness, pain, power and pride, poverty and weakness to might and brilliance

You are sailing into a time of good fortune and opportunity right now, and your dreams are right below the surface of the calm water you float upon. You are feeling emotionally sound, grounded, and in control. You know that you are protected and loved beyond measure. You are radiating positivity and power and feeling strong in your core of pure divine love. You are seeing evidence of your dreams manifesting before your eyes. The journey has not always been easy, and you have not always felt as secure as you do now, but you have defended your position and gained the upper hand with faith and steadfastness. Now is a season of success and opportunity, ease and grace, and you are well prepared to navigate the next steps on your path.

REVERSAL

Endurance, strength, hard protective exterior, adaptability. Storing resources, growth, optimism, moving quickly to prosperity, promotions, success, leading, steering a ship, harmony, cohesion, team dynamics.

Psst! Your strength and endurance are showing. You have firm resolve and are confident and ready to steer any situation to your advantage. The only reason that you might be feeling a little bit prickly at this time is that you have a firm resolve and a solid plan to take on the next leg of your journey. You've packed all the resources you need and have the ability to bring others onto your team. They want to follow you. If you have children, know that you are leading them comfortably and confidently at this time. You are the captain of this ship called life. You are speeding it forward into the sunlight and moving into a time of harmony, cohesion, smooth leadership, awards, and recognition. It's been a long haul, but your efforts have not gone unnoticed or been for naught.

UPRIGHT

Raise your vibration, deepen your connection with spirit, love and relationships, relationship harmony

You could be dreaming of a new relationship, or an upgrade to your current relationship. Send your intention up to the universe. What does this person look like? What qualities and traits do they have? Write a job ad for your ideal mate and hand it over to the universe. Focus on loving yourself in the meantime. Give yourself what you're seeking from someone else. If you're in a relationship and questioning how it could be better, send Spirit instructions and communicate with your partner, but this card indicates that you are heading for a relationship upgrade with new levels of harmony and understanding. You are surrounded by love, radiate love, and attract love. As you interact with others, you can expect your love meter to be filled. As you have given, so shall you receive.

REVERSAL

Take control, hidden opportunities, time of emotion, growth, releasing resistance, have faith, trust the process, stop comparing your progress to others

Hidden beneath what appears to be a dry desert is an oasis filled with opportunity. This can be a time that feels like it is heavy with intense emotion, but it is a time of beautiful growth, even though it might not look like it right now. Trust that the period of trials and difficulty will come to an end. This will not last forever. Go with the flow and release any resistance that you are holding. When we refuse to trust the ebb and flow of life, we end up staying in the tougher times longer. Admitting that things are not ideal and taking an honest look at how you arrived at this point are required to pull your head back above water. Take back your power, make necessary changes—no matter how small, and ascend the ladder to inspiration. Do not compare yourself to others. There is no comparison between any two life paths. Focus on your faith and know that this dry spell will end soon.

UPRIGHT

Communication with self and others, throat chakra, root chakra, cool, hot, activity, rest, balancing, differing opinions, misunderstandings, think through what you say

Communication is important. Think things through before saying them out loud, and consider your audience, especially when you are giving unsolicited advice. Steer clear of drama and gossip. There could be misunderstandings, and you are being reminded to consider that everyone sees things from their own unique perspective on the basis of their experience and perception of the world around them. Be clear, be kind, and use discernment, especially when it comes to electronic communication. Sometimes we can cause unintended damage with our words on these platforms. Think through what you say, write, or post. Have important conversations in person to avoid any crossed wires.

REVERSAL

People running hot and cold, boundaries, don't be a doormat, see from a higher perspective, resolving the world's dichotomies is not your job, conserve your energy

People around you may seem to be running hot and cold. Maintain your boundaries when it comes to what you will and will not accept when it comes to the way others treat you. Lovingly enforce your boundaries with compassion and understanding. This is not excusing bad behavior in others, but looking at them from a higher perspective. This card could indicate that you are trying to bring opposing forces into harmony, and wasting energy in the process. It is not your job or responsibility to solve any discord. Access your inner peace to bring you back to the present. Conserve your energy and allow others to be their own peacemakers. Know when to walk away, and trust that everything will work out for the highest good of all involved. Don't waste your energy on issues that don't belong to you.

CARD

UPRIGHT

Energy is picking up, new situations are brewing, people are looking to work with you and collaborate, but be careful about sharing your ideas fully. You are excited to get going, but you may end up speeding into a dangerous situation if you don't take time to plan ahead.

Your journey is blessed and your guides are working to see you safely to your destination. Your energy is rising around new projects being put in motion. Try not to burn the candle at both ends. Your career may be advancing or you may be starting a venture of your own. You're excited about the opportunities for advancement and bringing your desires and goals to fruition. Try to keep your commitments in check so that you do not overwhelm yourself or overcommit and underdeliver. You may have to rearrange your day and get up earlier to achieve your goals. Be careful about speeding into new situations without considering possible outcomes. You may race directly into the mouth of a smiling shark. Reevaluate, get all the necessary information, and look before you leap.

REVERSAL

People are watching you, people are looking up to you, integrity, walk your talk, practice what you preach.

Some of the best lessons and wisdom that we have are the insights that we give to others around us. It is necessary to remember that others are watching and using us as an example. Stand firmly in your integrity and practice what you preach. It's a bit like having children. You must always be conscious that others are watching your every action and listening to your every word (even when you have to repeat yourself twenty times) and using your example to formulate how they will handle their own life situations. Always strive to empower, uplift, and inspire others. Even if you don't see yourself as a natural leader, it's important to know that others are watching and following your lead. Even when nobody's watching, do what's right.

UPRIGHT

Meaningful connections, being nurtured, relationship with mother or mother figure, nurturing others, female relationships

This is a time to heal and nurture your relationships with women. You can expect new female companions to come into your life at this time. It may also be time to revisit or heal your relationship with your mother or any mother figures that are in your life. It is really a call for nurturing as the spirit of the Divine Mother holds you in her arms and cradles you. It is safe to take refuge here right now. If you are not feeling the need to take refuge and respite, give another person a safe place to rest. Rest and refuel or provide loving nurturing to those around you at this time. It is safe to close your eyes and dream.

REVERSED

Wisdom, message coming, retreat to receive, wisdom of the ancients, loyalty, primal drumbeats, roots

You have divine ancestral knowledge that is available to you at all times. You are connected fully to the stream of divine consciousness, running down from the heavens to the very center of the earth. Your roots run deep, and the wisdom of your ancestors and the ancients runs through these conduits and can provide great insight. The ancient ones are calling on you now to hear their call, seek some quiet, and listen to their wisdom. Look to the past for the answers. Maybe you have been here before. Trust the rhythm that beats within your chest. Sense the blood coursing through your veins. Know that Divine wisdom is readily accessible to you now. Have faith in your ability to conquer any obstacle that lands in your path simply through accessing your own divine wisdom.

CARD

UPRIGHT

Breaking away from the herd, striking out in an independent manner, your truth is out there, rapid growth, balance, comfort, finding your own answers

It's time to break away from the herd and explore the world in your own way. You've been feeling pushed to find your own truth because the life that you're living no longer seems to fit. The possibilities for your growth are endless, and your truth is out in the world. You'll find it when you look through your own lens and use your own experience and intuition to guide you. Do what your soul knows is right. When we do what feels good to us, we are led to new opportunities. Release yourself of the ties that bind you to the life experience and lens of other people around you. See the world in your own unique way. The world needs your perspective. Write, draw, paint, and use whatever creative medium you feel drawn to when it comes to documenting your journey. As you express your unique self in your own way, you will see new insights emerge and your path will become clear.

CARD 26

UPRIGHT

Power is in the now; stop ruminating on what was and concentrate on what is. Are you living or existing? The future is not promised and is constantly in a state of flux, so live now.

Your power is in the now. The past has already occurred. You can't change it, but you can choose to make peace with it. The future is not written in stone and is always in flux and flow. You hold the keys to your freedom by choosing differently. When you choose to sit and ruminate on the past and on things that could have been done differently, it is a waste of time. Pick yourself up, dust yourself off, note the lessons learned, and keep moving forward. Are you living this life or merely existing? You can choose to keep yourself in a place where you feel stuck, or you can choose to see the blessings that surround you and take required action. Trust your soul and know that the choices you make are the right ones. Your power is rising and you are feeling the need to pursue your inner dreams at this time.

Why are you still reading this? Get out there and live your life!

REVERSAL

Nourish yourself, body, mind, and spirit. Further education, ask an expert or mentor, acquiring knowledge rapidly through traditional means or a lot of life changes

It's time to nourish yourself, body, mind, and spirit. Take time to prepare healthful foods, hydrate adequately, and make time for meditation or reflection. You are feeling pushed to proceed, but you may feel that you do not have all the information required to make a decision at this time. Look at the resources available. Consult the internet or your community when it comes to available courses of study or books to read. It doesn't matter whether the means you use to acquire the information you require are of a traditional nature. It can be learned in a classroom, in a book, or from a friend or mentor. There's a network of people who are willing to guide and teach you. This could indicate that a mentor is on their way to you. Dr. Wayne Dyer always said, "When the student is ready, the teacher will appear." The time is ripe for learning.

CARD 27

UPRIGHT

Offerings, mysteries of spirit, rituals, wisdom and knowledge, seeking truth, awakening to divinity

Your guides, guardians, and departed loved ones are drawing near to make you aware of your connection to the divine. The divide that we perceive between the earth realm and the spirit realm is but an illusion that exists within you. You are free to connect to the spirit realm. Do not let fear hold you back from the pursuit of this ancient wisdom. Work with your spirit helpers. If you feel drawn to make an offering of herbs on your altar, or to light a candle in a church to honor your loved ones in spirit, go ahead and make this offering. They are making their presence and divine knowledge known to you. You are awakening to the fact that the ones we love are never truly gone, and that they are always here to bless and support us. Allow your connection to the divine to blossom. Ask for signs that you will understand and celebrate as they appear. Your connection to the other side is stronger than ever. You are beginning to understand that as you welcome spirit into your life and your everyday thought process, you are able to connect in ways you never thought possible.

REVERSAL

All experiences have value, obstacles conquered, success, joy, celebration of new skills, helping others, work with crystals for love, manifestation and protection, see your own magnificence!

All of your experiences have value, whether you perceive them as good or bad. With every obstacle that you conquer, you acquire a reminder of the lesson that was learned in each part of the conquering. These lessons are always carried on your person and make up the wonderful and beautiful person that you are as a result of the experiences you have come through. Acknowledge the wisdom that you've attained and the way that you can use this wisdom to help other people who may be going through similar experiences. You may wish to visit a crystal shop and pick up crystals that resonate with you, placing them in your home as talismans of love, manifestation capabilities, and protection. Know that you are protected, guided, and loved in all of your endeavors. You are getting stronger and wiser day by day.

UPRIGHT

Protection, alignment, dare to dream, letting your imagination take over, creating the future, going down the rabbit hole

You are making plans for the future. It's important to let your imagination run wild as part of this process. It's time to go down the rabbit hole of possibilities. Really have fun with it. Bring your vibration up and imagine all the roles you could possibly step into. How does each one make you feel? Does it fill you up and empower and inspire you, or does it feel disempowering? If it feels good, expand on it. What are the steps that will get you there, and what will it feel like when you achieve "it," whatever it is? During this process of imagining, you are creating a new and wonderful future. No matter what leap of faith you are considering at this point, you must know that you are coming into alignment with your soul's true purpose, and you are protected and carried by the angels. Take an exciting leap forward and bring the changes you have envisioned to life.

REVERSAL

Feeling out of alignment with spirit, examining what binds you to the material, releasing these bonds, embracing spiritual self and realization that there are many possibilities lying before you when you open your mind and bring them to your awareness

Are you feeling like a car with square wheels, just clunking along through life? You may be feeling like you have lost your connection to Spirit or that you are no longer aligned with your true soul purpose. Spirit wants you to closely examine what is holding you back and what binds you to the life you are living in now. The ego likes to keep us in a box and to hold us firm in the material realm. What has you chained? What are you attached to? Know that you have the ability at any time to cut the ties that bind you and keep you from your true spiritual nature. Spirit is calling, and you can see the light of one guiding star as a portal opens before you. Just imagine what is possible when you let go of your attachments and recognize yourself as a spiritual being. The whims of the ego and the material world will not matter as much when you embrace your spirituality. There are as many opportunities and discoveries before you as there are stars in the sky. Follow that one guiding star to a universe of ever-expanding possibility.

CARD 29

UPRIGHT

Judgment, legal matters, contracts, wearing a blindfold, missing half of the picture, see with both eyes, self-defense, self-preservation, read the fine print

Changes are happening fast. You're being asked to slow down, step back, and see the whole picture. Do not trust others blindly. This card can be indicating that there is a wolf in sheep's clothing in your midst at the moment who is telling you to do something so as to lead you directly into their trap. Step back and think critically. Use your inner radar to see the big picture with both eyes open. Remove your blindfold. Skipping this step could lead to conflict or even legal action later. Taking time to read the fine print is a method of self-defense at this time so you don't have to resort to self-preservation later. Especially when it feels like you are being pushed to sign contracts or purchase something, be cautious and understand exactly what it is that you are signing up for. Slow down and do the extra legwork now and save yourself some possible chaos later.

REVERSAL

Slowing energy after a time of conflict, showdown, loyal friends, dependable people, obstacles have been removed, celebrate your success, you have defended your point of view. Take time to heal, rest, and recharge after this battle of wills. Your light is shining brightly.

Whew! Been through the ringer lately? The energy around you is starting to slow down after a time of strife or struggle. You have stood and defended your point of view valiantly. The obstacles once standing before you have been removed, or you have convinced anyone who stands in opposition to you of your motives and why you need to take the actions you are taking. This can be a time where you have discovered which people in your circle are the most loyal and steadfast. They have helped you through this time and proven themselves as your allies, so keep them close. You know who your true friends are. Now is the time to put down your sword and rest. Allow your heart to be healed by the divine light of the universe. Spirit is working to repair any wounds or missing spots in your aura, and your energy will be replenished. The time of strife is over. Take time to tend your wounds and move forward with confidence.

UPRIGHT

Dualities, avoiding a situation or walking on eggshells around someone, stop procrastinating and do what you have been putting off, come face to face with stressful situations, resolution will occur when you use compassion, diplomacy, and inner wisdom

Avoiding a situation, person, or project at this time will not make it go away, and you may be enabling it to occur the longer you refuse to stand in your power and take action. The only way to truly know where things stand is to face them directly. You have the knowledge to bring things into the open, and you have the gifts of diplomacy, tact, and wisdom. Ask Spirit for help with finding the words if you need to, but they would like you to know that your success is ensured when you bring things to light. Have compassion and be gentle with everyone involved. Know that bringing these issues up will cut the tension once and for all and make the environment more comfortable for everyone. You may be involved in a team project where there are a lot of strong personalities and a difficult group dynamic. Use your voice and your leadership to bring the group together. Call out undesirable behavior in a kind and respectful way. Spirit knows you have this in the bag.

REVERSAL

Resting, reflecting, meditating, relationships with mothers whether on Earth or in Spirit, reconciling and coming to terms with these relationships, signs of love from a mother who has passed on, intention of becoming a parent yourself, focus on not trying to change others and accept them for who they are at this time

There is no love like the love of a mother. Please know that this bond transcends all of time and space. If your mother has passed away, consider this a hello and message of love from heaven. Meditate on your relationships with women around you, especially your mother, and understand that everyone is doing their best, on the basis of their level of spiritual knowledge at any given time. We do our best with what we have. This card could be an indication that you are thinking about becoming a parent. Rather than putting your energy in focusing on what you lacked as a child, or what mistakes were made, forgive and release women in your life from these grievances. Rather than trying to change others around you, focus on accepting them and loving them as they are. Just as the divine mother loves you unconditionally, give that same unconditional love to the people in your life right now. Understand the depth and breadth of how much you are loved.

UPRIGHT

Divine inspiration, ideas popping out of thin air, cooperation, coming together, common goals, teamwork, accomplishing more together

Do you have time for all these ideas that are popping into your head right now? As you are transforming, your thoughts are transforming and new intentions and ideas are being sent up to the universe at the speed of light. You are beginning to realize that it isn't about "me"; it's about "we" and how much more can be accomplished when we join with others in pursuit of our common goals. Start sharing your ideas. The more you talk about them, the more people you will find who would love to collaborate with you in pursuit of making shifts on a larger scale. The beauty is that you can accomplish more quickly with the assistance of others than you can on your own. This is a great time to take on new projects or collaborate with others. We can always accomplish more when we work together and combine our efforts than we ever will accomplish alone.

REVERSAL

Rocket speed, going with the flow, meeting opposing forces with a smile, a sense of community

The universe keeps moving, even when it appears that things are standing still. The world continues to turn and different opportunities are being set into motion. This is a time of rapid change. It might feel like the rug is being pulled out from under you, and you might crack apart in the process. This is part of the plan. It might seem a bit crazy to roll with all the changes that are being presented at this time, but you are being invited to do so. Meet any challenges or opposition that you face with a smile and determination. Choosing to look at things in a positive and cheerful manner can help you conquer them. There's no point in worrying. You know you have what it takes to conquer the day! There are always other people who are willing to lend a hand and support you when you need it, just as you may be called on to support and help someone else during this time. Keep your giving and receiving in balance and hold on. The ride might be fast and bumpy right now, but it's not going to stay like this forever.

CARD 32

UPRIGHT

Prayers being heard and received, talking to loved ones in spirit, your loved ones can hear you, live in your spiritual truth, see others with compassion, it's a sad life with no magic, miracles unfolding all around you

Spirit hears you talking to them. Know that you are able to entrust your secrets, hopes, and dreams to your guides, your guardians, and your loved ones in spirit. Trust that your prayers are being heard. Ask Spirit to orchestrate the changes you envision for yourself. Feel your power rising as you acknowledge spiritual truth and shed your old personalities, stepping beautifully into your power. Reach out to your favorite gods and goddesses or loved ones in spirit at this time, and know that they are there to assist you in achieving your best outcome. There may be some detractors to this process. There's bound to be people who tell you there's no way that it's possible to communicate with Spirit or that you're buying into "woo-woo" nonsense. Nod your head, see them with compassion, and go about your business. It must be a very gray world with no magic. You know the truth. Give up your concerns, unburden yourself, and live in grace and gratitude. Miracles are unfolding before your very eyes.

REVERSAL

Tough time, take a pause, no need to rush, alone time, self-care, worrying, breaking the cycle, meditating

Sometimes life gives you lemons. What do you do? Well, make lemonade of course! It could have been someone who was dishonest with you, or someone who disappointed you. Heck, it could just have been unfortunate circumstances, and you know these things usually come in threes for some reason. Is Mercury in retrograde or something? It's a good time to retreat. Take a pause and regroup. Instead of worrying about when the other shoe is going to drop (there is no other shoe), put your trust and faith in Spirit at this time, even if you feel forsaken. Meditate, focus, forgive, and flow. Take care of yourself and plan your next steps. Fade into obscurity for a short time until it feels like your feet have come back to the ground, if you feel that's what you need. We put high expectations on ourselves, and it can be difficult to realize we put the same expectations on others and they let us down. The only life you are in charge of is your own. Do what you need to do to heal and get back into the game when you're ready.

CARD

33

UPRIGHT

Bats in the belfry, what have you been putting off? You are on fire with energy and inspiration, massive creativity, take a leap, blossoming ideas and creativity

You are on fire with inspiration and creativity, but you are hesitating and waiting for the right moment to take action. Spirit is telling you that now is the time to blow the dust off those ideas that have been waiting for perfect timing, since there is no such thing as perfect timing. We never know what might happen tomorrow, so we are encouraged to live for today. Live your passion every single day. It may be time to make moves toward a new relationship or spice up your current one. Talk to your partner about what you need. Sometimes they need us to define how we need to be loved. New connections are blooming all around you, and the old bonds are strengthening. You will be supported as you step on the trail to new adventure and opportunity. Circumstances will align effortlessly as you follow your passion.

REVERSAL

Looking for comfort, family, been through a tough time lately with lots of challenge, wanting to see familiar faces of loved ones, finding comfort where you can, knowing that this storm shall pass

It's time to recover from the period of challenge you have just conquered. You are weary from what you have faced, and it has seemed to go on forever. Surround yourself in comfort now. Whether that is a warm bath, or spending time in your home or with your family, allow them to support you. Be gentle with yourself. What is done is done. Make peace with any outstanding issues and let them go. Know that the time of suffering or turmoil has reached completion. Nurture yourself and allow yourself to be nurtured by others. It's a good time to retreat to your nest to roost until things settle down and you are fully healed. Let your energy replenish before you go running back into the fray.

Understand the person in opposition to you. Change can be a long process. Aim for greater understanding and go from there.

REVERSAL

Doing what is expected of you, seeking independence but not knowing how to go about it, apathy, avoiding conflict

You may be feeling the judgment of your parents or elders. Whether you have had to come back home, or you are just feeling as if the opinions of what others think you should be doing are weighing you down, you are feeling the eyes of judgment right now. Maybe you are playing happy family for the sake of avoiding conflict, because you simply don't have the energy to argue. You're playing by the rules for now, but Spirit wants you to know that not all is lost, and you can regain the ground you have lost. In fact, when you set your mind to the steps at hand and you start releasing the judgment of what others say you should do, you will start to see doors opening. It's okay not to know the next steps, and it's okay to let things fall where they may. Remember that this judgment you feel is likely out of love. It doesn't make it acceptable, but consider the source. The people you want in your life are the ones who want what's best for you. Listen, use discernment, and then choose your own direction. If you are not feeling judged, take a heartfelt look at the way you may be imposing your judgment on others. Make changes where necessary.

UPRIGHT

Magic, manifesting, dreams, visions, shadow work, shadow self, a lot of energy to work on spiritual connection, there's no stopping you, determination

There is magic manifesting in the shadows. Even though things may appear dark, know that your pure core of light is burning brightly and sharpening your already keen intuitive skills. This is a time of great inspiration as the wisdom of the Universe is received. You can receive communication from many different supernatural sources, and you will be feeling very connected to nature. Your power waxes and wanes, but you are currently at a point of high energy and power. This is a great time to create an altar in your home with items that have a spiritual significance to you. Make sacred space and spend time there. Keep notes containing any information that you receive. It will be enlightening and useful. Write, create, and communicate while your energy is at its peak.

REVERSAL

Look beyond the surface, distractions, scavenging, dig deeper, scratching the surface, stop comparing yourself to others

Nobody is more enlightened than anyone else. We are all walking on our own path with Spirit at our side. Try not to look to others for validation of what you are doing. Know that you are exactly where you are meant to be at this time. Look deeper within yourself. Do not give up on your connection. Not all is lost. It may seem like there are distractions everywhere. Maybe they are things that you would rather be doing than deepening your connection or choosing to work with Spirit. It's not easy to acknowledge or even look at your own perceived flaws. Surrender to the process. It is okay to ask for help. We all need help from time to time, but don't compare yourself to others or convince yourself that you are doing it wrong and others are doing it right. There are a lot of detours on this path, and working with Spirit is never something that should be taken lightly. Commit, dig deeper, and hang on. This journey is going to pay off as you travel onward, open to the knowledge that lies before you.

CARD 36

UPRIGHT

Celebrating success, lessons learned, evolution, ignore the haters, new cycle starting, big things to come, always growing, always learning, keep going

You have ascended the mountains and learned the lessons required of you up to this point. You are being called to stop and look back at how far you've come. Give yourself a pat on the back and acknowledge the work you have done to get here. Look at who you were at the beginning, and see the amazing ways that you have grown through your experiences. You have accomplished great victories and lived through some crushing defeats, and used every part of your experience to learn, grow, and thrive. Love yourself then as you do now, and release the burdens of the past. Don't be discouraged if there are people in your world who detract from the growth within you. They may seem apathetic to your goals and aims. Who cares?! Celebrate the person you have been, the person you are now, and the person you are becoming. You are always evolving, growing, and learning. There is no destination on this journey, but the growth and maturity you have gained are measurable. Enjoy this moment at the top of this mountain; bigger mountains are ahead. This is the end of one journey. A new beginning is imminent!

REVERSAL

Seeing things clearly, removing illusion/emotion, you have more power than you think, new adventures, new journeys, reaping harvest, being comfortable with yourself, seeing what is

Are you seeing things clearly as they are, or are you seeing them through the lenses of some rose-colored glasses? As you begin to see with your soul and remove your emotions from the situation, illusions will begin to fall away and you will get the whole picture of what is really happening in front of you. There's a new journey unfolding before you, and you have the power to undertake it. You need to know that you are more powerful than you think. You're ready to hop on your trusty steed and gallop into the future. You have everything you need, and you are feeling self-confident and self-assured. You know that you are supported and loved fully as you take off on this new adventure. This will bring new people and opportunities that you may never have thought possible. You've already done all the planning and the planting of seeds. Your dreams and goals are manifesting in their brilliant glory, and you are free to set out on a new path. Reap your harvest and gather sustenance because this is the start of a long process; whatever you're pursuing, you're in it for the long haul. Don't worry and don't second-guess. You are prepared for any eventuality.

CARD 37

UPRIGHT

Pass on your knowledge, your experiences are valuable, create, be open to teaching and learning, share your wisdom

You are shaped and molded by every life experience. You are strong and independent, and you know that you do not have to rely on other people to fill your cup for you. Your legacy lies in the people you love and the life you create. All of us long to leave a legacy, something to tell the ones who come after us that we were here and that we made an impact. How are you transforming the world around you? What legacies are you creating? Spirit is asking you to keep creating. You are creating through all of your actions, whether it is caring for others or actually physically creating works of art or music, writing books, or sharing your teachings. What message are you leaving for those who follow you? Pass on your knowledge. Have faith in the ways that you are able to teach others. The best thing about teaching is that as you teach other people, you reinforce your own beliefs and open yourself up to new perspectives through the feedback you get from your students. You may learn something in the process!

REVERSAL

Psychic communication, premonition, connection, sending and receiving love and healing, powerful connection, good energetic flow

This card is all about communication. You are in a perfect time and space to communicate more clearly in the earth realm and in the spirit realm. Your throat chakra, which is your communication center, is open and flowing. You are safe to speak your truth, and you are safe and secure in what you believe. Not only is your communication awesome in the earth realm, but you are able to send thoughts and intentions out into the ether. Ever think of someone and they suddenly call you? The collective consciousness operates like dropping a rock into the middle of a quiet, calm lake. Your intention ripples through the entire consciousness until it reaches the one who is meant to receive the message. You are also able to send love and healing to other people across the realms of time and space with pure intention. How cool is that?

CARD 38

UPRIGHT

Breaking goals into smaller pieces to make them more manageable, don't let the ghosts of the past tell you that you can't achieve what you set out to do, slow and steady wins the race, cloak yourself in confidence

They say that if your goals don't scare you, they aren't big enough. You might be feeling overwhelmed by what you have set out to achieve at this time, and you might be worried that because you have "failed" in the past, history is going to repeat itself and you won't be successful this time around either. Break your goals down into monthly, weekly, or even daily bites if you have to. Check items off the list and celebrate your successes. You have all the resources you need for success, but you might just need to look at things on a smaller scale to keep them manageable and keep yourself focused and in control. Don't allow the ego to tell you that your ideas aren't worth pursuing. Set some boundaries when it comes to looking at the past. Know that that was then and this is now. These are different times and different circumstances.

Success and celebration will bloom all around you when the time is right.

REVERSAL

Confidence, style, sassiness, attitude, don't change to fit in, people are looking because they're missing what you have, adjust your entourage where necessary

The world needs your flair, confidence, and style right now. Don't feel like you need to change who you are to fit in. Know that the eyes that look upon you do so with admiration, and even if people are judging you, it says a lot more about them than it does about you. If they didn't care, they wouldn't be watching you. They're interested. They might even be envious. There's something that you have that they don't, and they are realizing their lack of it. Don't let it faze you. Just keep doing you. Walk confidently with your head held high. If others don't like it, tough. If you're feeling the need to step back from certain people who dull your sparkle and shine, do so. You are beautiful, you are strong, you are kind, and you are powerful. Own it.

CARD 39

UPRIGHT

Emerging from emotional drought, sun shining on all things, life-giving properties of the sun, new life, new direction, end of a cycle, dawn of a new beginning

The sun is shining after what might feel like a period of emotional drought. Whether it's because you've been putting off feeling your emotions, or you just haven't had the energy lately to deal with everything on your plate, the sun is beginning to shine again. Know that the sun is taking you out of a time of darkness and that you are seeing things in a new and brilliant light. The light is reaching all the corners, and you are able to get a full overview of life from a higher perspective. You are feeling the return of your energy and are beginning to feel more like your old self. Be grateful for the time you have had to spend gathering your resources. The old cycles have ended and your needs have changed. This required some time to process and get your thoughts in order. Taking this downtime where it was offered will serve you well as you march forward into new beginnings. Know that now you are ready to fully embrace a bright and brilliant future.

REVERSAL

Divine creativity, new opportunities, good fortune, ideas, revelations, inspiration, seeing the way forward, new jobs, new start, new opportunity, write, publish, grow

New ideas are sprouting up everywhere, and it can be hard to focus on one when there is so much inspiration everywhere you look. It's time to plan your next moves. It's a time of a lot of lightbulb or "a-ha" moments. You are capable of creating with ease, and the way forward is becoming clear as you focus and listen to the advice of Spirit. You are ascending to new heights when it comes to creativity and commerce. Put your ideas out there. The world needs your insight right now. Go with this amazing and creative flow. Embrace what your spirit and your soul are creating.

CARD 40

UPRIGHT

Don't put your head so far up someone else's butt that you forget who you are and what you stand for; the price this person is asking is too high

Be conscious of people of influence around you. It's time for boundary enforcement, since you may be getting too close to someone who is asking too high a price for their help or influence. You might think that they have it all together or that they have an edge you don't, and you want their participation in your projects. Maybe you are putting them on a false pedestal and are not considering your own emotional costs. Do not get so caught up in someone else's agenda that you forget who you are in the process. Be true to your own message. Keep giving and receiving in balance. If you find that your giving and receiving are not in balance, then step back and reevaluate so that compromises can be made if they are necessary. If the cost is too steep, walk away. Make sure that your energy output and mental and spiritual well-being are considered. Maybe the truth is that they need you more than you need them. You get one shot at this specific life. Ensure that what you spend your time on is worth your investment.

REVERSAL

See the potential your friends see in you, keep going, crush it, you have what it takes, it takes courage to do great things

Your friends are cheering you on and giving you a gentle kick in the butt to keep going. Keep working, keep pursuing your dreams, and keep reaching for the stars. In order for any kind of progress to occur, you have to keep going. It might feel like you are being pushed or nagged, but your friends want to see you succeed. See the potential in yourself that others see. Look at your strengths instead of your perceived weaknesses. Not seeing any strengths today? Ask your tribe what your strengths are. The answers might surprise you. Sometimes the only thing we need to keep us moving forward, no matter the pace, is a gentle butt kicking from our friends. It's easy to be complacent and do what we've always done. It takes courage and determination to truly manifest our destiny. Check in with your cheering section.

Conclusion

We are so excited to send this oracle deck out into the world and to see what insights, advice, and inspiration it can provide to others. Heck, we look forward to using it ourselves! When you open to your intuition, the world and your creative potential expand. New perspectives are always a source of power. They help us find clarity and regain control in times of uncertainty in our lives, reminding us that we are always participating in a cocreative partnership with the universe. Thank you for choosing this deck to be a trusted navigational tool. We wish you joy, luck, love, peace, success, and harmony as you cocreate your best life ever!